Narcissistic Stalker: Staying Safe And Fighting the Fear of Your Abusive, Narcissistic Ex

By Lauren Kozlowski

While every precaution has been taken in the preparation of this book, the publisher assumes no responsibility for errors or omissions, or for damages resulting from the use of the information contained herein.

NARCISSISTIC STALKER

First edition. April 20, 2021.

ISBN: 979-8201447540

Written by Lauren Kozlowski.

Table of Contents

Leaving Your Abuser: A Chapter For Those Still in a Narcissistic Relationship

If you've already left your abuser and are suffering from their harassing and abusive stalking, then please feel free to skip this chapter and head to the next chapter, *The Horrific Treatment You Endure at the Hands of a Narcissist*. This chapter is directed at those knowing (or wanting) to leave their narcissistic partner but are finding themselves feeling unable.

When I escaped from my abuser, I left with almost nothing. I had the bare minimum of everything: money, resources, support. I had been abused, trampled on, and gaslighted to the point I was in a constant state of fogginess, confusion, and anxiety.

Despite finding my strength to leave, and the strenuous planning it took to do so, I was still very vulnerable after leaving. I was susceptible to returning to the relationship if my ex caught me at the right time. I had blocked and deleted every avenue I could that he could contact me on, but I knew he wouldn't just let it end there.

No amount of blocking or running away would stop him from trying to control me, no matter how far away I fled from him. He was still there; in my nightmares, in my thoughts, and in the memories I was trying so hard to forget. This wasn't enough for him though. He wanted full control of me no matter the distance I purposefully put between us. It was his mission to overpower me with the fear he knew he instilled into me, and for almost two years, that's what he did.

He found out where I lived. He found out where my new job was. He knew what time I had my lunch break, and where I would go to pick up groceries. He found out my new number and tried various methods of contact to get in touch after I blocked him. He made his presence known by turning up to the same places I would be, and glare at me from afar. As much as I tried to not show fear, I don't know if that was possible given how scared of him I was. Sometimes he would try to speak as if we were friends, often in a menacing way. Sometimes he would cause a scene. Sometimes he would do nothing but look at me.

The fear of him and the fear of not knowing what he'd do would strike sheer terror into me, leaving me unable to think straight. I lived my life in a state of fear for two years because of a person who thought they had the right to control me and own me, and in the process of overcoming this, I found out I wasn't alone.

Being stalked by an abusive ex is scarily common. The stats and figures that show how many people are killed or hurt by an abusive ex are upsetting and angering to hear, but sadly, they don't surprise me. From enduring the stalking of my ex, to the survivor stories I have read, to the other men and women I've chatted to online who've been through this, I know the dark reality of being stalked. I know the fear. I know how alone it feels. I understand second-guessing every decision, being so uncertain of yourself.

There are few things in life that I can compare to leaving an abusive partner. The thought alone is anxiety-inducing, let alone taking the steps needed to go ahead and actually leave the relationship. More than this, whilst you know your partner is abusive, you still love them, which makes it feel almost impossible to escape the entanglement. To close your eyes and imagine a life where you're stress-free, able to live without fear or nervousness seems like a far-fetched fantasy. Whilst you may yearn to have the emotional safety, the calmness, and freedom that you can have without your partner, simply upping and leaving isn't an option.

What about your partner? What about the life you share? What about money - how will you survive? What about your family? What will happen to my spouse if I leave them? I won't ever be free of my abuser so I might as well stay. I'm too old/poor/weak/ insert-your-own-limiting-belief here to leave.

The fact that you're here, holding or listening to this book, means you (at the very least) know you're with an abusive partner. You might be a few steps ahead of this and are wanting to leave your nightmare spouse, or you might be teetering somewhere in the middle of this: Knowing you have a toxic partner but feel unable or unsure as to how you can be free of them. Wherever you are in your journey towards breaking the invisible shackles of abuse, this book is a good starting point.

The fact that you've sought this book out and are here right now is a step a lot of victims of abuse don't ever take (and if you winced at the word 'victim' and wanted to put this book down, I know how you feel - embarrassed, shameful, guilty... Whatever negative emotion it made you feel, override it. Keep reading. It's not a word to be associated with any negative feelings towards yourself. From a victim is born a survivor, and that's what I am; so if this book can give you anything, I hope it's the strength and tools you need to fight the fear and leave your abusive relationship.)

I had a seven-year relationship with a malignant narcissist. He was cruel, verbally and physically, and would manipulate, control, gaslight, and lie to me until I was nothing but a broken source of narcissistic supply to him. No matter what he put me through, what he said to me, how hurtful his actions or lies were, he knew I'd still be there when he decided that's what he wanted. If he went out for days on end, he knew I'd be sat there when he returned home, ready to let him slot himself back into my life again, which wasn't hard, considering it revolved around him.

I don't know your particular circumstance or what kind of abuse you've endured. You may have been subjected to lashings of verbal abuse, never being able to do or say the 'right' thing to your abuser. You may be in a stifling, controlling relationship where your abuser controls you so subtly that no-one but you could ever see it was going on. You may be with a physically abusive spouse who wouldn't think twice about striking you and then putting the blame on you for it. It could be that you're with a mentally abusive partner who lies, manipulates, and gaslights you into thinking you're going crazy. No matter what you're going through, I know it's tough. It's a hard thing to endure, and dare I say it, even harder to escape. But let me tell you a little about me, and hopefully, it'll give you the food for thought needed to devour the rest of this book and gain the courage needed to break free from the toxic bond you're glued to.

I was in an abusive relationship for seven years, which to some of you reading seems like nothing compared to how long you've been with your hurtful spouse. For some of you, it may seem like an eternity, and looking back at my time in this toxic relationship, it sure did feel like an eternity when I was going through it. Some people spend decades in this situation; others find their strength to leave much sooner. Regardless, the impact it has and the emotional effects it leaves behind remain the same, and wishing you left sooner or had found the courage earlier does nothing to help push you in the right direction.

During my seven years in hell, I was subjected to put-downs, uber controlling behavior, nasty remarks, and comparisons between me and other women. My abuser cheated on me, and although he would deny until he was blue in the face, the evidence wasn't hard to find. His infidelity wasn't just once, and it was almost like he didn't feel he had to cover his tracks, as he knew I'd take him back anyway. Looking back, I'm inclined to believe that he wanted me to find out, to hurt, to feel less than others, to feel degraded, all because it helped him in his ultimate cause: to control me, to know he had power over me, and to feel superior.

As well as the emotional abuse that saw him manipulate me, he would get incredibly aggressive with me, too. This would happen when he felt backed into a corner if I dared to confront him about his vile treatment of me. It would also happen if I did something that he deemed to be an insult to him, or if it made him feel like he was losing his grip on me. For example, if I went out and told him I would be half an hour, but I took forty-five minutes instead, not only would I get interrogated when I got home, it would often turn into aggression towards me. The same would happen if he found out I'd been talking to someone he disapproved of, or if I took a colleague up on an offer of a lift home, or if I got a text message off an old friend... The list of things that would ignite his rage is lengthy. His fits of aggression would vary in severity; sometimes he would smash things, punch walls, or break his own items.

Other times, his violence would be aimed towards me directly, and it wasn't one punch or shove (not that this is ever okay, I'm just stressing how hateful he was towards me) - it was prolonged episodes, and it was something I lived in a state of fear of. Sometimes, I wouldn't know what would set him off, but when the look in his eyes shifted and his expression changed, I knew I'd done something 'wrong' to provoke what would come next. It could have been what I said, or the fact that I'd mentioned someone he didn't like, or sometimes it could be a completely made up reason. He might tell me I said something (that I knew for a fact I didn't, but an abusive, manipulative narcissist can make you believe anything once they've snared you in their web of abuse.) Whatever it was, I knew the violence was coming when his demeanor changed.

His abuse was also emotional and verbal. He would tell me I wasn't looking good in comparison to other women. These women he would compare me to were women he worked with or knew, so it was done purposefully to make me feel inferior to these women he was interacting with. He would mock my appearance yet be derogatory and venomous with his words if I tried to make an effort. If I dared make an effort in how I looked, he would accuse me of doing this for someone else's benefit, particularly the male colleagues I worked with. He would accuse me of having affairs, or at the very least wanting to have an affair and his 'proof' of me thinking this was paper-thin, but he still managed to get me thinking that I was doing something wrong to make him think this.

He would often recount his version of a conversation with me and it would be full of things I didn't say, or he would twist the things I did say to fit his own warped version of events. He would scold me if I said something in front of other people that he didn't want them to know.

For example, one year we didn't book a holiday as funds were tight, and when we bumped into his friends one afternoon, the subject got onto summer holidays. I mentioned that we were giving it a miss that year to save some money, and the look he gave me pierced right through me. I knew what was coming when we got home; he accused me of embarrassing him on purpose, to make him look useless in front of his friends. I got called all the names under the sun and endured three days worth of silent treatment. I was just being honest with my ex's friend, but it got to the point where I felt I couldn't say anything in front of anyone anymore, as I never knew what I could or couldn't say. I was suppressed in ways most people can't imagine because they've never had to endure this kind of overpowering, repressive domination from their spouse.

Of course, the relationship didn't start out like this. The monster that I ended up spending seven years of my life with wasn't the same man I met in the first instance. The man I met put himself across as kind, caring, funny, and as someone who listened. This, sadly, turned out to be a facade, but by that point, I was already lured in and trapped in this toxic relationship. The warm, engaging, thoughtful man I met had gradually turned into a controlling, manipulative, hurtful, cold, inconsiderate, and cruel abuser who made me think his treatment of me was all my own doing.

After seven years in this poisonous relationship, I finally broke free. I must point out here that I'd tried multiple times before to leave without much success. I'd leave only to return to him again, with it often being me who would reach out to him to try and reconcile. Other times, he would convince me things would be better if I returned to the relationship, only to find I would be punished for trying to escape him. Regardless of my many failed attempts, the one that matters (and the one this book wants you to know is possible) is the last time I left my abuser. The final time, the one that made me cut the invisible cord tying me to my narcissistic, cruel tormentor. The one that, as difficult as it was to plan and carry out, was the starting point of me creating the life I deserved and healing from the years of abuse I'd endured.

If you're reading this, you might have tried and failed previously when leaving your relationship. No matter if it's been two or ten (or twenty) failed attempts, that doesn't mean this next time is the time. With a stronger mental foundation, a more robust outlook on how your life should be, and knowing that a relationship should make you feel safe, secure, and comforted, you can change the position you're in.

But I'm not ready.

But you're here, reading this book.

So, whilst you don't feel you're ready yet, you're readying yourself to make at least some changes in your circumstances. You're stronger than you think you are, and by seeking out books like mine, you're in a much better mindset to take back the reins of your life than you think you are. Trust me when I tell you that so few victims (there's that word again - don't let it define you, let it encourage you to rub out that word and change it to 'survivor' if it makes you feel shame) actually seek out help. Whether that help comes in the form of online articles, books, audiobooks, podcasts, support groups, social media pages... No matter what form it comes in, only a small percentage actually face up to what they're truly going through and even less seek out change.

You're more ready than you think you are.

Here are some things I think may also show you're in a position to read this book and utilize it as you're supposed to.

You're ready if... You've stopped pretending everything is okay.

For such a long time, the mere thought of telling my parents or long-lost friends the truth about my relationship ate me up. I would shake that thought out of my head almost as soon as it popped up. I was ashamed, and having to admit what I'd been going through (through my own fault, or so I thought) was enough to keep me trapped in the nightmare of a relationship.

What would people think? I'd be the talk of the town, with all my friends gossiping about how I picked a dud, or how I was lying about the abuse, or how I provoked it.

As the abuse escalated and I became more and more vacant, some miracle caused me to search online about abuse. The shell of a being, the living, breathing emotional zombie I'd become, searched desperately for some kind of refuge from the way I was feeling. I can't remember the exact phrase I searched for, but it took me into a rabbit-hole of information about domestic abuse, narcissistic abuse and emotional manipulation. From here, with my eyes opened somewhat, I devoured everything I could about abusive relationships. It took a little while, but the head-in-the-sand approach eventually stopped working for me. I knew I was being abused. I had the courage within me now to admit that to myself.

You're ready if… You know your abuser can stop, but is choosing not to.

I let myself believe that my abuser couldn't help himself or his abhorrent behavior. His childhood, his relationship with his parents, his dysfunctional views about relationships, the way his ex had treated him, the childhood traumas… I found, for quite some time, that I was blaming his abusive treatment of me on everything but the true proprietor of the abuse: him.

Because of my instance at deferring the blame to anyone but him, I didn't label his behavior as such. As most people do, I told myself I would never remain in an abusive relationship. This was different, because my partner was damaged. What kind of partner would I be if I upped and left a traumatized man when I could be understanding and try to help him?

The harsh truth to my empathy was that no matter what he'd endured or what kind of childhood he had, he carried out his vile treatment of me because it gratified him. It gave him power, satisfaction, a sense of importance, and the ability to feel like he mattered so much because I remained with him regardless of what he did. My kindness and sympathy was rewarded with him taking advantage of that and abusing my good nature to fuel his own sadistic quest for dominance.

I stayed with him because I loved him, because he made me believe that he'd been hurt, and I truly believed that eventually, love would conquer all. Little did I know at the time, love cannot beat down the walls of narcissism or manipulation. That is a battle that can't ever see the empathetic one win, because sadly, that's like trying to stop a substance abuser from using your love. An addict won't stop using their drug of choice because you love them and plead with them. Their love for the drug will ride higher than their love for you. And, in this case, an abuser doesn't hold any genuine love for their victim - they only love how they can make them feel.

Alas, I stayed with my abuser because I'd been beaten down by years of insidious treatment and constant guilt trips, and, eventually, I didn't believe I deserved any better than what I was getting.

It took a while to wade past the smoke and break the mirrors he'd manipulatively put up. But, once I did, I uncovered a difficult truth; he could stop his vile treatment of me. He just didn't want to. He didn't abuse me because of his childhood, because of his problem with alcohol, or because of the questionable people he associated with.

He did it because it satisfied him. If you've come to realize this, or are able to take this fact away and accept that your abuser is willfully choosing to treat you so disgracefully, then you're ready to make some moves in changing your life. This is a hard fact to digest, but once you do, it's fuel you can use to keep you empowered.

You're ready if... You're prepared to trudge through the drama of the aftermath of the breakup because you know the payoff will be worth it.

This is a difficult place to get to. Often, we stay with our abuser because the idea of breaking it off is too frightening - we fear the reprisal of the abuser, and we stay for our emotional (and physical) safety. You might not quite be at the 'prepared' stage when it comes to enduring the aftermath of the breakup - but I'm going to assume that, at the very least, you know the payoff will outweigh the drama of the aftermath.

Think about being offered the choice of the red or blue pill in The Matrix (even if you've never seen this film, the below analogy will still work.) I've never seen The Matrix myself, but when I was given the 'pill' analogy, it helped me put my feelings into perspective:

The blue pill means you'll wake up and your life will remain the same - no additional drama or stress, but you're still in your relationship. If you take the red one, you'll wake up having already left your partner, past any of the breakup heartache, drama, pain and complications.

The theory is, those who choose the blue pill want to keep working on their troubled relationship. Those who chose the red pill may be realizing for the first time that they are not in the relationship just because they love their partner. They are still there because they fear the breakup and all that comes with it.

I'm guessing you've just carried out that mental experiment on yourself (if not, do it now and find out which pill you'd take - the result may make you understand if you need to continue reading this book now, or to put it down until you need it, or make you realize you'll never need it.

If you're living in the hopes your partner will change...

Let me tell you that the abuse will keep happening. Even with your love, help and support, abusers have deeply rooted emotional and psychological problems. Although I can agree that change is not completely impossible, it's certainly not quick or easy (or without the abuse you're looking to escape from). With your love, care and best intentions propelling you, you want to try and better your spouse. However, change can only ever happen once your abusive partner takes full responsibility for their behavior and wants to seek out professional treatment. This also means they dig deep enough and stop blaming you, their sad childhood, life stresses, work pressure, addictions, or their 'uncontrollable' temper.

If you think you can help your abuser...

I get it. I was there at one point. It's only natural that you'd want to help your spouse. You might think that you're the only person in the world who understands them or believe that it's your responsibility to fix their issues. But the harsh truth is that by staying and accepting the repeated bouts of abuse, you're actually reinforcing and enabling their behavior. This is a difficult concept to comprehend, but by staying, you're not helping your abuser, you're maintaining the problem.

If your partner has promised they'll change...

When faced with the consequences of their actions, abusers will often plead for another chance, beg you for your forgiveness, and promise to change. It's believable, too, but their true goal is to stay in control and keep you from leaving. Most of the time, they'll quickly revert back to their abusive ways once you've forgiven them and they aren't worried about you leaving.

If you're worried and anxious about what will happen to you or them if you leave...

Then know that this is a natural feeling.

You may be scared of what your abusive partner will do, where you'll end up, or how you'll support yourself or those dependent on you. But, please - don't let fear of the unknown keep you locked up in a dangerous, unhealthy relationship.

I want you to keep those four points at the forefront of your mind, and don't be enveloped in those emotions when it comes to leaving. Easier said than done, I know, but it's important that you don't weigh yourself down with debilitating thoughts that are driven by your feelings.

Our brains have the capacity to amplify anxiety. You understand the drama and aftermath of ending the relationship can turn ugly. But, by sitting down and working through the finer details, you come to see that you can craft a plan. You see that it is doable.

Let me mention something else here: your abuser will likely notice you finding your strength, and they will view this as you separating from their control. It will undeniably unsettle them, and in this situation, the abusive behavior tends to heighten. They will want to make you pay for daring to regain some strength, or for having the audacity to push back on the abuse.

I implore you to stand firm in who you are, begin to grow the roots of self-respect, and fight for the future you deserve. Writing this from the perspective of a survivor, I can promise you it'll be one of the best, most courageous, scary, empowering, life-changing decisions you'll ever make.

Choose the red pill. This book is here to help guide you through the aftermath. To those who've already taken the red pill, you've done it. You're braver and more powerful than you'll ever know. Let's move on to the main focus of this book and talk about disarming a narcissistic stalker.

The Horrific Treatment You Endure At The Hands Of A Narcissist

One of the most manipulative things a narcissist does is reel you back in time and time again. No matter how horrific their actions, how vile their treatment of you has been, or the number of unforgivable things they've said, a narcissist has the ability to coax you back into the relationship time after time. It was the same for me, too; I can't remember the number of times it took me before I ended the relationship for good. It's well into double figures without a doubt.

The way a narcissist can lure you back in is like nothing you've ever experienced before; somehow, they can make all of the abusive things they've done fizzle into nothingness, and you're just happy to be back with them. A lot of the times I left my abusive ex, I'll admit it was me who made the first move at reconciliation. I would flee the relationship when the toxicity, abuse, and hurtful treatment of me got too much.

Many times I would do this with no true intention of leaving for good; in the back of my mind, I just wanted my ex to miss me, to see what he had and what he was ruining with his horrible behavior. However, even when my ex showed no signs of remorse or guilt, I would be the one to extend out the olive branch. Despite him being the one who behaved so terribly during our relationship, the dynamic of an abusive relationship doesn't follow 'normal' relationship rules. When you're under the control of a narcissist, you're not thinking logically or about what's in your best interest. You are bound to your abuser, feeling powerless to do anything about it except endure it and hope one day it'll be different. No matter how evil and malicious their treatment of you, the abuser often doesn't need to do too much to tempt you back to the relationship.

Before I talk about the way a narcissistic abuser behaves after the relationship has ended, I want to discuss how they treat their victim in the relationship. If nothing else, this chapter will make you remember just how awfully you've been treated. If you're still with your abuser or have tried leaving but find that you keep returning, this chapter can serve as a primer to you gathering up the strength and willpower you need in order to make some proper, permanent changes. Whilst that's an easy statement to make, but a very hard thing to actually do, don't underestimate your own inner strength and power; I've been free of my abuser for years now.

It took multiple attempts, a lot of soul searching, ugly feelings, and a lot of self-discovery, but I'm the best I've ever been in life. Physically, emotionally, spiritually, financially... every way in which my abuser suppressed me, I'm now excelling in. It's why I'm able to write this book with such passion in regards to life after abuse; it's a difficult journey to navigate your way through, but the payoff is undeniably worth it. I want to guide you to take that journey and have the mindset to really break the chains of abuse. In order to do that, you need to confront the abuse. Wherever you're at in your abusive relationship now - whether you're in the middle of leaving, if you're enduring the hellish stalking of your ex, or if you're reading this in anticipation of leaving your abuser, this chapter will give you a little jolt towards doing what's best for you.

I was verbally and physically abused. I was told what I could and couldn't do, who I was allowed to talk to and who I had to avoid. I was ripped away from my family and close friends. I was told I was stupid, worthless, ugly, fat, braindead, a waste of time, a pointless vessel which served no purpose. I was thrown out of my own home countless times, physically. I had numerous black eyes, bruised legs and arms, cut lips, and lumps on my head. I lived in a state of fear for eight years, with each passing year, the abuse getting worse and worse. I'm going to describe the methodical, malignant ways in which a narcissistic abuser treats their victims, and not only may you see your own situation reflecting in some of them, it will also help validate your feelings about the abuse being so wrong.

Abusers have a way of being able to manipulate you to the point that you normalize the abuse in your own head, and when you accept the blame for everything that goes wrong in the relationship, you begin to diminish your own hunch that this relationship is toxic. When you get to this point, it helps to hear the stories of others who've been through the same kind of abuse. It can help chip away at the gaslighting and brainwashing that the abuser has so meticulously been carrying out.

I'll discuss the main aspects of the horrific treatment a narcissist exposes you to in a little more detail below:

Gaslighting

You've likely heard this word before, especially of late. It seems to have become a buzzword of sorts, which isn't necessarily a bad thing, as it's drawing attention to a hidden form of abusive manipulation. To strip back this method of abuse in order to explain it simply in one sentence, gaslighting is essentially the abuser pulling their victims strings and making them question their own memory, recollection of events, make them doubt their own perceptions and judgment, eventually causing the victim's self-esteem to drop to dangerous levels.

My abuser would tell me I'd said something, even if I hadn't. Despite the fact that, deep down, I knew I didn't say whatever he accused me of saying, he'd still get me to believe that I'd said such a thing. One thing he accused me of saying is that I'd leave him for someone else if he went to visit his cousin in another city for a few days. I'd never, ever said this, but he got me believing that I did - and that's the cruel, controlling power of a narcissist. The irony here is that this sentence is something he would say to me, not the other way around. In hindsight, he made this up so he could 1) tell me he was going to his cousins and try to make me feel anxious the entire time he was away, and 2) make sure I was going to sit at home whilst he was out having fun.

The list of things my ex said and did to gaslight me is vast, but after years of enduring it, I really did feel like I was going mad. Instead of questioning myself, "Did I really say that?" I would just accept his version of events. I would no longer rely on my own judgement or recollection of events, because I didn't trust them anymore. If my ex didn't come home until the early hours of the morning, he'd tell me, "I told you I was going out! Why do you have to act like I didn't tell you? Just so you can act all crazy and upset?" Of course, he didn't tell me he was going out. He'd just go out then tell me he'd told me he was staying out late.

He got me to the low, low point where I thought I was losing my mind. My reality wasn't real - it was a reality he'd created, and it was utterly confusing, upsetting, and totally disorienting for me. But, of course, this is what he wanted. Does this sound familiar?

Cheating

My abusive ex was also a serial cheater, not that he would ever have outright admitted that. However, it didn't need to - the evidence was always there, usually. From finding messages on his phone, to him hiding his phone when it pinged, to him taking off for days on end only to return when his new target had had enough; there was always some trail he left behind to evidence his cheating ways, but he would never admit it.

Even if I caught him directly in the act, he would still have had the audacity to deny it. This ties back to gaslighting - he would feel like he could convince me he hadn't cheated even if I saw it with my own eyes.

The cheating would happen with women he worked with, or women he met when he was on a night out. As a narcissist, he would relish in the idea of these women then pining after him when he returned home, and would keep in contact with them as 'backups'. Sure enough, if he wanted to go out and meet one of his backups, he would instigate an argument or accuse me of something ludicrous. This would then give him the green light to storm out of the house to retreat to his 'family'. After a while, I found out he never (and rarely did) go to his mother's or brother's house when he stormed out. He would go drinking or meet one of the women he kept in the background.

Narcissists are prone to cheating because they crave the adoration and validation that this gives them. They need to feel like they're 'in demand', and will seek out other partners despite being in a relationship. Should a narcissist ever confess to cheating, it's more likely to be to get a rise out of you than it is from a guilty conscience. They need you to know they're in-demand, that they can get someone else at the drop of a hat, and that you're lucky they're with you. And, because of the way in which a narcissist builds a trauma bond with their victim, it's unlikely you'll leave them after an admission of cheating.

Whilst my abusive ex never admitted to cheating, he didn't hide the fact that he did very well. I knew he cheated and had messages from women who also confirmed this. They knew too much and told me too many accurate things to be merely trying to cause issues - even if they were trying to cause issues, their stories were certainly true. Regardless of this, I was so scared of losing my spouse that I stayed. I believed his lies, his gaslighting, his manipulation, and his abusive reasoning for everything.

Physical Abuse

An emotional abuser is often not averse to physical abuse, too. While not every narcissist or abuser gets violent, more often than not, they do. Emotional and physical abuse go hand in hand, and physical abuse doesn't just mean black eyes or bruises.

Shoving, purposeful rough treatment or aggressive actions towards you all count towards your partner being physically abusive. Restraint can also be a form of abuse. The narc will confine you by blocking a doorway for example, or forcefully grabbing you when you try to leave. They might lock the doors and remove the key, or go as far as tying you up to stop you from leaving.

This, quite intentionally, causes a horrible feeling of entrapment and imprisonment with no way to escape. Because the abuser has already demonstrated (through their isolation of their victim) their ability to cut a person off, physically restraining you becomes a hint of (or rather, a promise of) further aggression. When this happens, it's a warning to get out of the relationship immediately. As we know, though, rarely do we see the warning flags waving in our face.

Verbal Abuse

Narcissists often use the tone (and volume) of their voice to covertly establish dominance over you. They can do this via two extremes - one, by increasing the volume of their voice by screaming, yelling at you and generally raging. The other extreme is equally effective: they offer complete silence. You'll be ignored and your spouse will refuse to respond to you. Their tone, should they offer a response to you, serves to reiterate their hold over you. Their petulance (and often their pompousness) will make you do anything for their forgiveness or compliance.

We know that words have meanings way beyond their definition - they can be used to instill fear into you, intimidate you, manipulate your thoughts, and oppress your desires. Threatening language and nastiness often comes easily to the narcissist when their victim refuses to act how they want them to. Should you try to use the same method against the narc, their verbal assault upon you will simply amplify.

A narcissist's speech is frequently argumentative, sarcastic and demanding. They will often interrupt, speak over you, hold back important information, and bully you while they interrogate and probe invasively. The shock of verbal assault feels so cutting and is delivered so rapidly that you don't have the energy to fight it. This is what the narc wants.

Personal attacks like name-calling, mockingly berating your feelings, and judging your responses will deflate you. To add to your confusion about being attacked, the narc will slyly mix some truths in - with a whole heap of criticism. This abusive tactic leaves you feeling not only inferior but also defeated.

A narcissist does whatever they need to in order to avoid feeling embarrassment, including being uber defensive over minor misunderstandings. Their self-perception is so skewed and twisted that they frequently accuse you of trying to make them look bad. When they think you're attacking them, they become hostile, invalidate your feelings, lie, and conveniently forget commitments they've made.

Narcs are also masters of the blame game; anything that happens to go wrong is the victim's fault. They accuse you of being way too sensitive, are overly critical and dismissive of others' reactions and opposing opinions. Essentially, the victim is the one to blame for the negative conditions in which they find themselves.

Do these sayings feel familiar?:

I'm critical of you for your own good.

I was only joking when I said that, you can't take a joke!

If only you would do_______, then I wouldn't have to be this way with you.

That (abuse) didn't really happen like you describe it.

As a result of constant verbal abuse, you feel like you can't ever win. You're always in the wrong, resulting in a loss of self-esteem and self-confidence. You're forever walking on eggshells, you're fearful of your spouse's response to your thoughts/actions and often find you're embarrassed by their behavior.

Suppressing You/Controlling Via Manipulation

Manipulation is a reliable behavior of a narc. Manipulation is a key tactic used to achieve their end goal: control.

With love has to come vulnerability. In the right, loving, caring hands, our self-doubts, flaws and insecurities are respected. We feel safe enough to be ourselves. However, in the hands of a manipulative person, our kindness, vulnerability and love are taken for granted. These things are used against us, twisted to fit our abuser's desire to exploit them. This manipulation can be seen directly or covertly, but, regardless, the intention is the same.

To control and hurt.

It hurts to comprehend that your abuser is using your personal feelings and sensitive information to destabilize you. The purpose of it - to gain control - makes it all the more upsetting.

Direct and indirect manipulations are utilized to keep you close to the abuser - to keep you attached. Their exaggerated, dramatic tales are meant to maintain your attention, particularly if they feel it's slipping. Please understand that these tactics aren't because the manipulator loves you and wants you to stay. It's because they fear your love, attention, and attachment to them are beginning to wane.

When I first sought help for my trauma due to a narcissistic relationship, I was told to think of the relationship between yourself and the narc as a rope. The rope was once coated in something that was attractive, comforting and soothing. It was enticing, manipulative and coercive enough to entrap me into thinking the possession - the rope - was love. As the relationship evolved, the rope slowly but surely got tighter. The manipulator was slowly gaining full control.

As the rope's tension increases, the warm yet deceitful covering begins to fade away. Once a warm comfort, the rope now begins to chafe and burn against your skin. Manipulations, lies and occasional love-bombing are used to recover the ropes' sheath'. This stops it from snapping, thus preventing you from getting free.

Narcs can't accept the idea that another person doesn't want to be with them - they can't handle rejection (or what they perceive as rejection). Keep in mind that one trait of a narcissist is an overblown ego and a deep-rooted belief that people are envious of them. They won't accept the possibility that their partner can live happily without them. If the narcissist loses the loving attention and affirmations of their greatness from someone that was previously well-controlled by them, they'll go to extreme measures to regain that control via manipulation tactics.

Certain methods of manipulation are unashamedly brash, and are used purely to incite empathy from their victim. Some narcissist's won't think twice about threatening suicide or saying they have a plan for their suicide. The sole purpose of this shocking statement is to awaken the caretaking traits in their victim and keep them close.

I'll Be Watching You: The Stalker Ex

You probably know the feelings all too well - leaving your house and checking the area to see if there's been any signs of your ex being there. If they've left you a 'gift' or some kind of calling card. Or if you're shopping, you feel a sense of unease about them popping up just to stare at you from a distance. If you're out with friends or at a social gathering, you have knots in your stomach at the thought of them turning up to cause a scene.

If, God forbid, you're on a date, you make sure you only go to places you're as sure as you can be that you won't be seen. The sick feeling in your stomach when your phone rings and the number is unknown. The dread you feel when you get a text message from your ex despite blocking them. The panic that overcomes you when you find a note pushed through your letterbox that's filled with threats and accusations. There are dozens upon dozens of examples I can use from my own experience here, but you get the gist; the stomach-flipping feeling of knowing you're being watched, checked up on, and monitored by someone dangerous is about as fear-inducing as it gets.

For two years, that was my life. I lived in a perpetual state of fear and worry, unsure of what my ex's next move would be. When I first left the relationship, I made sure there was no way he could find out where I was going to be living. I cut all ties with everyone who I thought would go back and be his informant. I chose a quiet area to live in and my house was the second from last on the street, which was a dead end. You had to drive through a few winding roads to get to my new house, and I was confident he wouldn't be able to find it. I made sure I drove home from work different routes each evening, just in case he was watching - I needed to throw him off the scent. At this point, my daughter was living with my mother whilst I sorted our new way of living out.

I was doing a good job of concealing my new living arrangements by being vigilant and extra cautious about my movements (which meant my abuser was still controlling me from afar, but I was scared for my safety and my future.) Then one day I had a parcel delivered to my house that I needed to sign for. I had let my guard down a little by this point, having not seen my abuser for a couple of weeks, and his abusive messages had started to wane a little. I used to peek through an upstairs window before answering the door, but my unease had dropped to the point where I could now answer the door from behind the chain. When collecting the parcel I was expecting, I opened the door and looked up; to my utter horror, the delivery driver was one of my ex's friends. I had no idea he delivered parcels as a side job. My heart sank into my gut, then I wanted to bring it straight back up out of my mouth. As friendly as this man was, I knew without a doubt that he would run straight back to my ex and tell him he saw me - and my new house.

Later that night, as expected, my phone pinged. It was my ex. *You didn't move as far away as I thought you would.*

At this point, I had gone through stages of blocking my ex's number, to then unblock it. For years, when I would leave him and go to my mothers, I would block him then unblock him, but it was different then. I would unblock him so we could reconcile. This time, I was serious about leaving for good. I would unblock him so I could keep an eye on the abusive threats and accusations he would message me. Not only would this be kept to use as evidence if I needed to go to the police, but it also helped me keep abreast of how much he knew about me and let me know what kind of things he was planning. For example, he messaged me once to say he would be outside of my work at 5 pm - I told my boss who let me leave at 4 pm. If he was still blocked, I reasoned with myself, I would have walked straight out of work and bumped right into him.

When I got the message from my ex telling me in so many words that he knew where I was living, I felt helpless. I felt like there was no escape. I even thought about going back as it was a case of 'better the devil you know'. I felt a lot of conflicting emotions, I felt anger, I felt upset, I felt guilt, I felt stupid, I felt weak, I felt like I wanted to end my own existence because that would be the only way out. This then began my two-year living hell of being stalked by my ex.

I wrote a timeline of the stalking down as a way of documenting it. I didn't begin this straight away; however, I spent the first few months after leaving my abuser feeling too helpless, hopeless, and broken to do anything proactive or forward-thinking. I was in such a daze after leaving, logic and rationale seemed so far away.

September 2012 was the month I left my abusive ex. It was months in the making. I'd planned it as much as I could. I did everything I was advised to do online; I gathered up my important documents, I copied the ones I couldn't hide from my abuser, and I created a separate savings account that my ex had no idea about. This planning began as far back as January 2012, but I needed to save as much as I could and get everything in order before I could leave.

Most of all, I needed my own place. I couldn't retreat to my mother's again - not only was she beginning to get sick of me leaving my abuser only to return, but I could also tell she was sick of me in general. It was almost as if she too was blaming me for the abuse I was enduring. This really didn't help with my self-esteem. So, this time, and to make sure I didn't return, I needed to be renting my own property. I was in no position to buy one at that point. So, for months I saved as much as I could without my ex knowing, and I compiled a folder of all the important documents I would need: passports, tax documents, bank statements... Everything I could put together.

I spoke with my daughter before leaving. I'm lucky that we have a pretty open relationship. I told her a few weeks before I left that I was planning to and that she would be staying with her grandma for a little while as I sorted our new life out. My daughter was quite close with her father as a young child, but as she grew older, she began to see him for what he was; mean, nasty, and a bully. She called him out on it sometimes, too, and his efforts to control her (when they weren't blocked by me) were deflected by her. She was 12 when I left, and understood why I had to leave. She knew she couldn't stay with her father as he wouldn't have been able to take care of her. The relationship she once shared with my ex was ruined by him and his abusive ways; he burned their bond by purposefully exposing his daughter to his cruel ways.

I left at the beginning of September at sometime in the evening. My daughter was already at my mother's house. I had a bag of clothes and some essentials. My new home was barely furnished, but I had enough in the bank for another two months rent. I still had my job. I had no friends, my mother seemed disgusted by me, and I had no one to talk to. But, now, I had myself, and that was something I'd not had for a long time. As soon as I left, I drove for an hour or so before heading to my new place. I cleared my head a little and blocked my ex so I couldn't see the abusive messages come through. My ex wouldn't go to my mother's to try and find me unless he'd been drinking - he needed to be drunk in order to confront my mother. Even then, he would back down, but not before throwing something at her window before leaving - he was childish and petty, and this was his style when losing an argument. I knew my daughter was safer there, however, and once he realized I wasn't there, he'd look elsewhere.

It was then he began calling my work, but I'd told my boss I'd left my partner and gave her a brief overview of him being abusive. At the time, I didn't feel comfortable divulging the whole truth, but he understood enough to know that my ex was a danger to me. When my ex realized he wouldn't get to speak to me by calling up as himself, he would either give a fake name or get one of his friends to call up, then pass the phone to him. This was unbearably embarrassing at the time, and I know that my ex just wanted to exert his control over my emotions no matter how much distance I put between us.

Things remained the same for me the majority of the following year. My ex would leave empty beer bottles at my doorstep, he left a random voodoo doll on my car windscreen, he posted me letters - some were beyond abusive, others were telling me how much he loved me. It was utterly anxiety-inducing. He would use his flying monkeys to spy on me. He would text me and tell me things I'd done; for example, when I got a lift home from work, he would message me to ask who was dropping me off. Another time I came home from work to find kick marks all over my front door. He was very clever in avoiding doing anything that would incriminate him.

The stalker ex also uses emotional manipulation on you to keep their tight grip on you.

They'll create elaborate lies up to guilt-trip you or invent emergencies to gain your sympathy. After all, they know you're the kind, sympathetic type, and they've always been able to use your kind emotions against you before to get what they want. They might send you messages like, "Why are you putting me through this? All those times you said you cared were just lies. You're just like everyone else." These emotion-inducing tactics from the stalker ex aren't from the heart. They aren't heartbroken they've lost you - they're upset they've lost their narcissistic supply. They're mad at the thought they've "lost". They're incensed by the idea that you had the audacity to leave them - don't you know how great they are?!

It's also common for a stalker ex to make empty promises to prolong contact. Example: "This is the last time I'll be in touch, honest." Of course, it's not the last time. Often, they'll promise a "last contact" when utilizing the above manipulation tactic, like "Did you ever love me, really?", which can prompt you to respond. They know how to get to you. This false promise is just another way to get what they want.

Another vile tactic they use is to resort to blackmail, regardless of how far of a stretch it may be. The blackmail may even be something that isn't true. Or, it could be holding something they've told them over you. For example, they may threaten to expose a secret of yours or do something to sabotage your job (which my ex actually did, although unsuccessful). You would be surprised as to how far a narcissistic ex will go when they're faced with rejection. Their stalker behavior post-breakup can cross boundaries you didn't really think they were capable of. If anything, let it affirm just how right you were to get out of the relationship. You need (and deserve) so much more.

The stalker can also play on your deep insecurities, ones that you told them about and offered up in great trust. You didn't make yourself vulnerable like this for them to use it against you, but the jilted narcissist will use this as their ammunition to get a rise out of you. They will use your self-doubt and fear and play on these things to make unfounded accusations. They're prone to twisting your words to suit their malignant agenda. "Remember when you said you'd always love me? You're a liar!" Again, twisting things to maintain their own narrative is standard narcissist behavior, so it's important to be aware of it so you know to block it from your natural urge to reply or explain yourself.

A stalker ex can often give expensive or elaborate gifts in an attempt to lure you back - but these gifts have heavy strings attached. Should you reject the gift, you'll be met with comments about "ungratefulness" and "all they've done for you", but you know better. It's a trap. A one you've likely fallen into too many times before. Promises of change or gifts to express how sorry they are have previously been met with the acceptance and obenance the narc is used to. When these things no longer work on you, the narcissistic ex will hurl all sorts of hurt towards you, using their knowledge of you to get to you as best they can. Don't let this work. Don't give in, don't feel like you need to explain yourself, and block the imminent feelings of guilt (as you've been conditioned to feel). You owe your abusive ex nothing.

Why Us? The Traits a Narcissist Seeks in Their Victim

I had a lot of guilt and shame when I left my abuser. Most of it wasn't for leaving, although I did have a few moments of feeling jolts of guilt about that. The majority of my guilt and shame came about because I felt foolish. I felt like I was an open target for my abuser. I thought that I was stupid, gullible, so obviously naive that my ex saw me coming and took that opportunity to suck me in. I was filled with anger and blame, all directed towards myself. Some days the anger towards myself outweighed the anger and resentment I felt towards my abusive ex.

For almost two full years, I questioned, 'Why me?' I couldn't come to any other conclusion that the abuse inflicted upon me was all my own doing. It was my fault for just being me: dumb, annoying, incapable of being someone who people can care about, and so worthless that I deserved the treatment I received. I think back to the self-hate and pity I so regularly engaged in and I wish I could somehow go back in time to show my former self this chapter. Never did I imagine then I'd be writing this book, let alone this chapter (where I'm most certainly not placing the shame and guilt onto myself anymore).

After much internal conflict, reading up on why people abuse, and slowly regaining my sense of self, the realization hit me: I wasn't to blame. I wasn't a defective human, only deserving of subhuman treatment. Sure, I was targeted by a narcissist because of certain characteristics of mine, but these traits were things normal, caring, decent people would cherish in a partner, not take advantage of.

Narcs benefit from certain traits of yours. These include:

Your forgiving nature.

Narcissists most certainly benefit from being with people who forgive them for being so hurtful, cruel and upsetting. If you weren't so forgiving and gave them chance after chance, they'd not be able to have their full grasp over you. A narc's other half needs to be forgiving by default, otherwise they risk the possibility of rejection - and they despise the thought of being rejected. The narc will continuously hurt you, and they know that - they fully intend for that to happen in order to soften you up to further manipulation. In order for them to control their spouse, they need to be with a person who won't hold grudges; or at least, bring those grudges up and rebuke their promises not to behave so poorly in future.

Your unwavering loyalty.

Emotionally inadequate, insecure and mistrustful individuals, like narcissists, require loyalty from their other half. Bear in mind, this loyalty is a one way street; it's not reciprocated. Many narcs will fully demand loyalty from their partners, putting great emphasis on how important it is to them. All the while they'll be hypocritically betraying their loyal partner themselves; often by cheating, lying, crazymaking, backstabbing and being generally deceitful. All of this occurs with no remorse from the narcissist.

This hypocritical stance needs to be backed up by your other trait:

Your ability to overlook the bad and see the good.

You frequently see the good in people. For every bit of bad someone exhibits, you'll be able to see past that and acknowledge the good. Victims of narcissists often have the empathic trait of being able to overlook people's bad actions or traits, allowing the good to shine through. If the narc is bad tempered, the ability to see past it to other things such as generosity, humour or comfort is something the narcissist banks on. Every person, no matter how much bad they've done, has some good traits; even the most abusive of monsters have glimmers of good. The fact that you can see this is an attractive quality to the narc. Not because it shows how compassionate you are for your fellow human being, but because it benefits them. They can utilize it and capitalize on it.

You have an external locus of control.

Simply put, targets of narcissists are frequently people who aren't self-referencing, but instead are others-referencing. In layman's terms, they don't look internally for their decision making, by asking questions like, "How am I feeling about this?" Rather, victims of narcissists make their choices by how the other person might react to it. This selfless decision making wholly benefits the abusive narc, with their spouse having little concern for themselves when considering their actions.

It took me a while to accept that I had an external locus of control. I assumed it meant I was weak-willed, had no thought for myself and was self-destructive. In essence, this means that

I had no belief that I was in control of my own life. I wasn't, for the most part, but the fact that I could regain control of it seemed too out of reach to contemplate. I was berated, ashamed, depressed and a shell of who I was before I met my partner. I felt well and truly rock-bottom, so to comprehend that I was in fact in control of my own destiny seemed too much to accept. It's this belief that you can't control your own fate that a narcissist clings onto and exacerbates.

You can be self-sacrificing.

Partners who are self-sacrificing are attractive to narcissists. These abusers don't have much (often any) desire to focus on their victims' wants or needs. They need a partner who is willing to put their needs on the backburner - indefinitely. Whatever hopes, dreams, aspirations their victims once had must be cast aside if it doesn't match what the abuser wants. This way, the abuser can always be sure they're number one and being taken care of.

Your giving nature is something the narc can't be without; your willingness to sacrifice your own desires puffs up the narc's sense of worth.

You're responsible.

Without realizing it, you probably tend to take on the responsibilities of others quite a lot. Since narcissists are irresponsible (emotionally and otherwise) having you there to pick up the pieces helps keep them keep the cycle of abuse going. After all, someone needs to pay the bills/look after the kids/ clean the house/keep them fed/etc. You take on a parent role when you get sucked into a relationship with a narcissist, taking care of them without expecting much in return. Simply being with the person you love is enough for you.

You're extremely accommodating.

Abusers must have their own way - or the consequences are too upsetting to even consider. Narcissist's are often controlling and rule-orientated in their expectations of you. They are utterly inflexible in this department. It wholly benefits a narc to have a partner who is willing to go with their flow and not make a fuss over anything - at all, ever.

If you are extremely flexible, happy to not get your own way and willing to compromise your desires and needs, then you are precisely what a narcissist seeks out.

***

I must stress these traits that I've just outlined are good traits. You're kind, empathetic, open to forgiveness and understanding. You can see past abhorrent behavior to get to the good. A decent partner would appreciate this without taking advantage of it.

You still can possess these great traits, and you absolutely should - but you don't have to allow another person to exploit them. You don't have to be forgiving, unwaveringly loyal, self-sacrificing, overly responsible, and so accommodating to someone who doesn't appreciate and value these traits in you. This is wisdom and discernment.

But what is wisdom and discernment and how do you implement it?

Wisdom, as you know (because you have plenty of it), is the lessons you have learned from life's experiences. You're here reading this because you have already become wise to the ways of your abuser and are looking to expand your knowledge. Put simply, in exchange for the negative experiences you've been through, you've gained wisdom. You have a deep understanding of what it's like to be in a relationship that's toxic, soul-crushing and exploitative. Wisdom gives you the advantage of being able to think before acting.

This is where discernment becomes involved. Essentially, it's making choices based on wisdom. Once you realize that your kind traits are being used against you and your partner is using them to manipulate you, you can use this knowledge to make decisions regarding who you'll demonstrate your good traits to in future. Use your hard-earned wisdom to spend your good traits only on those who deserve it and will use them with good intentions.

Narcissistic, Abusive & Toxic; But Why Do I Miss My Ex?

Before I delve into why you might be missing your ex despite their deplorable treatment of you, let me answer another question you may be thinking of: *Does my ex miss me?* Isn't their behavior just their twisted way of expressing their skewed version of love?

Let me answer that. **They're not missing you.**

They're basking in, relishing in, feeding off of the fact that they're controlling you from a distance and being able to retain a big chunk of your thoughts.

Before you read this chapter, I want you to dissolve any thoughts you may be having that your abuser is 'missing you', therefore showcasing this in their typical, cruel ways. You may begin to feel pangs of sympathy, guilt, shame, or you might succumb to thinking that your abuser can't show heartache any other way, so they stalk and harass you. This might lead you to revert back to old thoughts of being able to fix or soothe your abuser, to help them mend their ways and evolve into a happy, healthy, stable human. If these thoughts have crept into your mind, you need to zap them with a dose of reality. Let me clarify what that reality is once more:

They're not missing you. They're basking in, relishing in, feeding off of the fact that they're controlling you from a distance and being able to retain a big chunk of your thoughts.

Now we've established that your abusive ex doesn't pine for you because they love and miss you, let's tackle why you may be missing your ex. There are five main reasons, and I'll outline them for you below:

1. You're suffering from Stockholm Syndrome.

I go over the effects of Stockholm Syndrome in my book, 'Trauma Bonding' in more depth, but a quick overview of this syndrome is that it's a psychological condition where a victim of abuse develops a deep empathy for their abuser.

You end up doting on your abusive partner so much so that you end up justifying the episodes of abuse and don't want to leave them. If you do manage to get out of the relationship, the trauma bond can often remain intact. This causes you to grief for the relationship, to deeply miss your abuser and pine for them. You probably stayed in the relationship for as long as you did because you couldn't imagine ever being without them, regardless of how horribly your partner treated you.

This emotional attachment to your partner means that you've found yourself somehow justifying or forgiving every abusive deed, often citing their poor start in life or past traumas of their own as the source of their behavior.

'They were bullied in school', 'they had an abusive childhood', "Their mother died at an early age', etc. will be prevalent in the victim explaining away the actions of their abuser. Since the abuser has already showered their love upon you, effectively love bombing you, it will be hard for you to associate their actions with the truth - that they're an abusive manipulator. It's understandable that you feel this way, and more importantly, it's normal. You're empathetic and caring, it's in your nature to believe and forgive. You want to 'fix' and 'mend' your abuser, seeing the best in them; but sadly, this hope is misdirected. It's never going to happen.

1. You find yourself missing the good times you spent with your ex.

We both know that abusive partners are not abusive in the beginning. Imagine if they were? They'd not be able to lure any poor victim into their trap. Instead, they love-bomb, they manipulate covertly and they hide the most sinister sides of themselves until it's too late. You're already entangled in their web. You kid yourself that the person you met - the loving, charming one - is the real them. You stay with them hoping the 'true' them will return. While dating, a narcissist spends a good amount of time showing their love to their partner before revealing their cruel true colours. You choose to believe in those moments of love and happiness while to your abusive ex; it was just a ruse to get what they wanted.

The good times throughout abusive relationships make you believe that the abuse isn't permanent; you believe you can change them and get back those precious, far-away happy moments. But, there's no question of them changing for you. Your partner's traits are baked in; it's who they are. They love-bombed to get the desired outcome.

2. Your partner endured a traumatic past.

All of us have our share of bad times throughout our lives. We all have our traumas but at different intensities. It could be that your ex has experienced more trauma than you have. Because you loved and adored them so much, you believed that their abusive behavior was their way of reacting to and coping up with their trauma. It's the way a lot of people think; traumatized people, traumatize people - hurt people hurt people.

But no matter how much trauma anyone has gone through, it's inhumane and cruel to make others suffer for it. Please understand that it's not right to justify harmful behaviour or actions by past trauma. If your ex had issues coping with trauma, you were fully there for them, to support them and be there for them. Help is out there, and taking out on you - the one person who would do anything for them - is utterly a glimpse to their true person. It's cruel, it's abusive and it's pure torture for the person on the receiving end. You are not here to be a punching bag for someone else's pain, no matter how much you love them.

3. You feel like everything is your fault.

Typically, in abusive relationships, the abuser makes their victim suffer from bouts of shame and guilt. They go out of their way to make things look as if it's all your fault, heaping blame onto you for things that couldn't possibly be your fault. You don't forget these feelings easily, and even after you've left the abusive partnership, these old feelings remain. To burden the blame for things has been your way of life for so long, it's almost second nature. You might feel like you're the reason the relationship went the way it did and you might find at times you're ashamed of the way your ex acted because you feel you have some responsibility for it. Despite your ex's cruel treatment of you, their manipulation and blame towards you makes you think that the breakup is your fault. So, you begin to miss your abusive ex because you harbour belief that they are not responsible for it - you are.

4. You still believe things could have been different.

It's easy to sink into daydreams of how things could have been different, how nice your lives could have been and how great you were together. A lot of this is rose-tinted hindsight, and thinking about how it could have been is a one-way ticket to getting back in touch with your abusive ex to regain some of that familiar comfort. You fell in love with your narcissistic ex because of the apparent good qualities you saw in them. They were "perfect". Even now, you may find you still believe that maybe things could have been different had you not acted in certain ways.

***

The purpose of this chapter is to show you the importance of stepping back, coming out of these thoughts and understanding (and believing) that you deserve to be loved back. You can't just give, give, give... especially when the taker is constantly doing just that. You need reciprocation in a relationship. You need to feel safe. You need to feel secure, loved and wanted. Being abused, afraid and riddled with self-doubt is no way to live. Yes, it's natural to miss your abuser. I did. I missed having company, someone to watch films with, someone to hug, I missed the good times, even though they were tainted by the all-too-often bouts of abuse. But, you need to look at your emotions with a clear head. You can't remove the happy memories that niggle you, but you can rationalize them. Don't let yourself be manipulated by your own emotions - it means your ex's conditioning of you has worked.

You miss them - but you deserve better.

Will They Ever Leave Me Alone? How You Can Handle a Controlling, Stalking Ex

Being harassed by your abusive ex feels like purgatory. It's a repetitive cycle that you just can't see a way out of, you don't see how it'll ever end. You can almost resign yourself to living life this way forever; being controlled, suppressed, fearful, anxious, and afraid of the future. You know yourself: it's no way to live.

But it's also hard to see a way out.

For a long time, I only ever envisioned two ways of escaping my abusive ex: either he would go too far and end up fatally hurting me, or I would end things myself. That's how bad it was. For you, this may not be the case; perhaps you don't fear your ex will kill you, but you still fear there's no way out of this living hell. I used to sob to myself, "Will he ever just leave me alone and allow me to live a peaceful life," praying my abusive ex would just get bored and leave me be.

You can live in hope your ex will get bored and move on to another target - although the guilt that you've let them latch onto someone else is often too much to bear. In my case, my ex met someone else yet still hounded me when he could, albeit a lot less than before.

For too long I let my abuser control me from afar. I huddled up in a ball, hid myself away and tried to wait it out. I wasn't proactive in protecting myself from my abusive ex. When I left him I did so boldly, but I neglected to future-proof the onslaught of abuse. In hindsight, I could have done a lot of things better and faster, but I hope you can learn from my mistakes (or rectify the ones you might be making now). I want this chapter to guide you through taking control of the situation and handling your stalker ex.

First thing's first: Please, tell a friend, a relative, a coworker or your doctor what's going on. Tell someone. Even if you don't have a huge support system or feel like you want to tell anyone, it's in your best interest to do so. I get that it can feel daunting and you feel embarrassed about divulging this kind of information (especially if your stalker ex is good at hiding their tracks and you feel like you won't be believed).

But, opening up about this is a significant step. Not only are you breaking your silence - which is a step towards breaking free from the invisible hold your ex has on you - you are putting things in place to fight your corner should your ex do anything that requires you to get the police. I told my boss when my ex was stalking me and not only did it make me feel empowered afterwards (despite me being sick with anxiety before telling them) but it helped me feel a bit more secure in being believed. Looking back, if I'd told more people, they wouldn't have judged me or talked about me behind my back the way I thought they would. My big fear was not being believed, so if you feel this way too, it's very likely a symptom of being abused by your ex. They've conditioned you to feel unsure, to doubt yourself and to fear the worst. Take power back by speaking up.

If you can, talk to your family and friends. I was limited in this department, having few friends left and a mother who wasn't very understanding. But I reached out to old friends and people who I'd cut off or stopped responding to (because it pacified my ex). Despite expecting to be told how I was a bad person and an awful friend, most people replied to my reaching out in a positive way. I even met up with some old friends, who I still keep in touch with now. I was honest about why I cut them out of my life, and was honest about how guilty and stupid it made me feel.

You probably feel like you want to keep the whole situation to yourself, but what does that achieve for you? It's only enabling the stalker to continue with their vile behavior. Building a support system is a significant thing you need to do, no matter how small it is. A doctor, counselor or a person of trust at work are great first steps.

Don't do what I did and keep the stalker unblocked. Block and report - these functions on social media are your friends in this case. Block their number, their email address, every avenue of contact - cut it dead. Keep all threatening, incriminating and abusive messages but then make sure to block them. I kept my ex unblocked out of fear - I wanted to know how much he knew, what his next move would be and hoping his messages would help me work out his next move. This was wrong, though, and it only served to make me anxious, ensured I lived in fear and was afraid to look at my phone.

You need to cut off all channels of communication. This may mean enduring some minor inconveniences, such as changing your email address or your number. In the grand scheme of things, doing this is a small hassle compared to exposing yourself to the onslaught of mean communications your ex is firing your way. Fresh starts may require you to do things like this; you're not going out of your way to rid yourself of your abuser, but rather going out of your way to find peace and mental clarity. You're doing this for you.

Try to keep your address private. In my case, I lived in such a small city that my ex found out within a few months where my new address was. It was a stroke of bad luck that his friend delivered a parcel to my new home and went back to tell him where I was living. However, part of maintaining your safety means doing your best to place a barrier between you and your abusive ex. In the end, I moved to a city not too far away, where I got a new job (prior to moving) and lived month to month for a year or so before getting back on my feet. This isn't something everyone can do or even wants to do. So, if I'd stayed in the same city as my ex, I would've still done everything I'd already done to protect myself. I still go back to that city every now and then to see friends and family, and I've bumped into him and seen him around. None of these times has resulted in me speaking to him or me getting any correspondence from him, from a mix of me setting my firm boundaries, seeking a support network and blocking him. I have new social media accounts, so if he really wanted to, he could find a way to message me, but even if he ever does, I know what I can do: Block and report.

My advice, though, is to make your social media profiles as private as can be. Not just for the benefit of your harassing ex, but for those who are inclined to stalk your profile and report back to your ex (these are called 'Flying Monkeys' - more on these in the next chapter). All my profiles are as private as possible, and I'm still diligent as to who I accept on there. A big thing to do is to also change your passwords on anything your ex had access to, even if you don't believe they had access to it - we can be surprised at how sneaky a narcissist can be, often leaving us shocked as to how low and devious they can be. To be safe, reset passwords for everything; banking, email, and social media.

Cyberstalking is definitely a thing - your ex doesn't need to be waiting outside your house staring through your window. In this case, you should set your social media profiles to private (or make them as private as you can). Your ex could very well try to get in touch with you through fake accounts - mine sent threats from multiple fake accounts - and by doing this, you will undermine them by having a private profile.

Make a habit of keeping detailed notes of everything your ex has done. Even if you think it's not relevant or not "serious enough" to note down, diarize it still. It will be helpful if you ever need it in the future. This rule isn't one you can skip: document everything. Write down every single conversation, log every unwanted call, every text, email, or comments on social media. Even note down any comments from their flying monkeys, even if you don't deem it to be threatening, or even if you think they've managed to hide their malevolent intent well - detail every single thing regardless. I can't stress this enough. You might well find it ends up useful in the future.

Write down the date, the time and a description of every incident related to your ex making a presence in your life. Include what your ex did and what you did or said in response, and keep the corresponding messages if applicable. Any letters or presents left for you ought to be kept too; I took pictures of the random things my ex left on my car or on my doorstep. These pictures had date and timestamps.

Save copies, print outs and screenshots of every online interaction with your ex. Even the ones that might show you snapping or replying in a way that you might find embarrassing to show to others; you need to document warts and all. This will benefit you in the long run. I had a folder locked away in my wardrobe that was dedicated to all of my evidence. Every time I got an email, text or letter, I'd put it in the folder. I was even so paranoid (or perhaps worried is a better word) that my ex would break in and destroy all of this evidence that I backed up on my computer, too. My advice would be to make hard copies of everything as well. Be proactive, not reactive in this situation - which is great advice I didn't always follow myself. But for you, I implore you to live by that rule when dealing with your stalker ex.

It's also really important to note everything you do to address the situation. If you've confronted your ex, describe the situation in written form. Get screenshots of proof of you blocking them. You will need this detailed evidence if you decide you need to go to the police - which, I would advise you do anyway. Even if you don't want to go through with any charges at the moment, you can contact them with the situation and they can advise you what the next steps could be for you. Getting in touch with them will make you feel much more in control of the situation, because you will be.

Showing your evidence to the police will make your argument extremely credible if you want to proceed with a restraining order, too.

Some people advise confronting the stalker if you feel it's safe to do so. This, to me, is extremely poor advice. It's better for you - and sends a much clearer, more consistent message to your ex - if you stop all communication dead immediately. Sure, you might have moments where you blow up and reply to their antagonistic messages or reply to messages out of fear, but don't let this be the norm. It's what they want.

If you decide not to go to court about the stalking, there are some protection options available to you. Utilize these things; you come first. You need to be in a clear, healthy frame of mind not only for you but for those around you. You can't let a toxic, narcissistic ex win by giving them your energy and thoughts. Remember, this is what they want. Withhold that with all your might and spend it on things that matter.

Consider a restraining order, which is designed to keep dangerous people away from you. I can't give you specific advice on this due to the law being different depending where you are in the world - different states and cities have varying laws on this so I don't want to offer any incorrect information. I would suggest you look into the specific laws on this where you are. For me, there was an online form to fill out and after checking I was eligible for a non-molestation order.

While it is often used to protect against physical violence (they use "domestic abuse" as the name for the abuse on the form but it's also applicable to stalking), even if your ex hasn't escalated to violence, don't let this put you off seeking a restraining order out. Remember, violating a restraining order is a crime in itself - if they come so many miles or feet near your property or work (or whatever rules are imposed in your particular restraining order), you can feel secure if they breach them, knowing the police can pick them up for this. Even if police don't have enough information to arrest them for stalking you, they can still pick them up for not abiding by the restraining order.

Even if you don't want to go down this route, please check the rules on this for your area. Just knowing the criteria for taking out a non-molestation order is a benefit to you. Knowing the tools are out there, should you need them, will make you feel like you have more cards up your sleeve should your stalker ramp up their malignant behavior.

Here's a checklist of sorts for you to keep in mind when deflecting the unwanted attention of your stalker ex moving forward:

Be firm in any correspondence you offer (although I advise none). If you do reply to them, let them know you're unwilling to continue contact. Then, block. Don't say you won't be contacting them again, only to message them when they've done something upsetting or have said something to provoke you. This only encourages them. If you've already done this (and I'm guilty of it, too), you must now quit responding and avoid taking their bait. Silence is your friend here.

Please, please, don't worry about hurting their feelings. Abusers seek out people like us because of the traits I mentioned earlier (forgiving, loyal, self-sacrificing), and they will use these against you as much as you let them when you break up. They know they can get to you, and they know you're sensitive and they know they can manipulate you to the point of you caving in to their requests. Remember, when you left the relationship, it was their horrible behavior that prompted this. It wasn't an easy thing for you to do. But, they caused it - all they had to do was treat you with respect. That's all they had to do. If they had, the situation would have been very different. But, now you have to set boundaries to protect yourself.

A reminder to be mindful and vigilant about what kind of personal information you're putting out there when you post online and be wary of what you let your friends tag you in. I know, it's not ideal having to be doing this instead of being carefree about what your posting online to those closest to you. But, you need to be proactive, not reactive at all times. It won't always be like this, and you'll know when you can relax on your vigilance, but please don't hand your abuser anything you wouldn't want them to know.

Don't allow any apps to show your location. My ex could track my location from my phone, with my permission, during the relationship. When I left, I had to get someone to help me turn it off - I'm not tech-savvy, and even after this app was disallowed and deleted, I still felt paranoid about it somehow working (of course, there was no way it could). However, I read an article about a woman installing spyware on her husband's phone to track his movements, as part of an experiment to highlight how easy it can be for abusers to track their victims. Stay vigilant.

Keep your home, car and garage locked at all times. Make it super hard for your stalker to gain entry if they choose to overstep those boundaries and try to get access to your home. I knew my ex had the potential to try and break into my property, and made sure it was fortified as much as possible. I had the most secure locks, I installed security cameras, I had hidden cameras near the doorbell, I opened my blinds so you could see out but couldn't see in, I had an alarm fitted... little by little, I made my space secure. Even though he vandalized the outside a few times, I made it safe for me on the inside. I went to the police about his damage to my house and the evidence against him was irrefutable. I made it so he couldn't get to me - I could fix what he did to the property.

Think about alternating the driving routes you use. To work, to the gym, to go shopping, to your friends house... Don't give your ex a predictable pattern to be able to find you. Since I lived in such a small city, I made a point of mixing up my routines, changing them frequently so my ex couldn't find me. I started work earlier and left earlier. Sometimes, I'd start later and finish later, when my boss allowed (since I'd opened up about my situation, this was allowed). Don't offer the narc your routine. At times, I thought, "I'm sick of going out of my way just so he can't abuse me." But, instead of letting my defiance get the best of me, I put my safety first. I made it hard for my abuser to track me. I was the one "winning", because they were obsessed with getting to me - and they weren't. They were the ones chasing their tail, relentlessly stalking someone who'd left them. Quite pathetic when you put it into perspective.

Be wary of threatening to call the police and then not doing it. It turns into a case of crying wolf. Your ex won't take this threat seriously if you keep putting it out there but don't take action on it. Don't say you're going to call the police unless it's a genuine comment. Ideally, don't tell them even if you are going to call the police - just do it. Not following through with what you say will signal to your stalker ex that you don't mean the things you say - including that you want no contact.

It's hard at times, but keep cool, remain firm, and stay as calm as you can to avoid feeding into your stalkers desire to evoke an emotional response from you. Think about reacting before you do. Once you've rationalized things in your head for a while, you'll see that responding isn't the best idea. It's like an impulse purchase - instead of buying something immediately, take some time to ponder if you really ought to make that purchase. More often than not, you don't.

Don't try to minimize the stalker's behavior. After a breakup, you might find you suddenly start bumping into your ex at random or unexpected places or perhaps your ex just happens to be driving by when you're leaving work or you've spotted them more in the past week than you would have normally. At first, it seems odd that your ex is popping up so often, but lots of us simply shrug it off as coincidence or bad luck. You might even think you're imagining things or being "paranoid" (as I was told I was). Don't try to explain these oddities away like this. Even when we know someone's track record and patterns of behavior, it can be incredibly easy to downplay the potential risk they pose to us. Because of this, a stalker ex's actions can be dismissed as more of the same wicked behavior. But it's not - the situation has now changed: A narcissistic stalker ex is much more likely to escalate their behavior when they think they've got nothing to lose.

Please avoid trying to play the psychologist when you ought to be protecting yourself. Don't be drawn into their problems, their problematic childhood, personal issues or other excuses as to why they behave the way they do. Do not be drawn into promises of change. Do not burden yourself with their issues; they are not yours to solve. Getting sucked into the role of psychologist instead of protecting yourself only spells trouble. Plus, when you try to "fix" the abuser, it's all part of their game. They know you have a well-meaning desire to help them and this means giving yourself to them no matter the cost to your own well-being. They don't take your desire to help them as an opportunity to change, even if they tell you this. Keep this in mind when you want to "help" the abuser.

Avoid the belief that being stalked is your fault or something you're responsible for. It says so much more about the abuser than it does you. The blame game will cripple you. "I should have spotted the signs and known he was beyond abusive", "How could I have gotten entangled with someone like that? What's wrong with me?" Self beration is your enemy here, which means it's an ally of the abuser. The honest truth is that none of us can know what our partner will do once the relationship comes to an end. Don't beat yourself up with blame or "could have, should have" thoughts.

***

The history between you and your ex can tempt you to make mental mistakes that unwittingly put you at great risk. The bottom line of this chapter is that you have to be vigilant throughout this tough period. I know it's a difficult thing to endure, and your anxiety has been tested no end through this ordeal. Avoid psychological blind spots, avoid being reeled back in by emotional manipulation and as much as possible cut contact.

Swatting Away the Flying Monkeys: The Narcissist's Recruits Who Do The Dirty Work

If you've seen the Wizard of Oz, you'll know how the Wicked Witch had an army of nightmare-inducing flying monkeys at the ready to do her villainous bidding. It just so happens that flying monkeys tend to do the work for narcissists as well. A narc's flying monkeys are their "henchmen" - offering their unwavering support and helping the narc prop up their warped idea of reality. They help keep the narcissist's ego inflated and aid them in continuing with their self-centred behavior. After a breakup with a narcissist, you want to be on the lookout for their henchmen doing their dirty work for them. If you're reading this book, you may already have had a run-in or some trouble with a flying monkey.

The narcissist's ever-faithful henchmen are rarely ever willing to see how the narcissist's actions and behavior are affecting you. Just like their narcissistic leader, flying monkeys are well-versed at gaslighting you and denying your reality, frequently getting involved in triangulation (which is a manipulation tactic where the narc communicates directly with their follower, using them to relay communication to you, thus forming a toxic triangle) and gossiping about you.

All of this keeps the narcissist happy by generating a lot of chaos, and you may find that your stalker ex relishes in the 'smear campaigns' they spearhead (as well as other ways of humiliating you). The flying monkeys are firmly allied with the narcissist, seemingly enjoying the drama of it all. But, flying monkeys aren't always so brazen and open about their desire to upset you or offer you up to the cruelty of the narc - some even pretend to be your friend in order to obtain information from you. This information is then fed back to your ex. It's hurtful to think that perhaps those you deem to be friends could wish ill upon you, but it's a sad fact of dealing with any narcissistic ex, let alone a stalking one. Be wary of "mutual" friends you share with your ex; use your gut to determine their intent and don't offer up an abundance of information that could be used against you.

It's important for you to recognize the flying monkeys for who they really are: gaslighting enablers. They can gaslight by proxy; for example, you may mention that you've had a rough time with your ex. They could respond, "They're not that bad, I've only seen good things from them," making you feel as if you should doubt your own perception of your ex. Hearing things like, "They've never behaved like you describe" or "They mean well" feel like a dagger to the heart when you know the truth.

The gaslighter-by-proxy is essentially doubling down on your ex's manipulation and by justifying them as a person.

Meanwhile, it's important to look out for "gaslighting by group." This is when multiple people openly doubt your reality with your ex and support the narc. Red-flag phrases can often start with the word "we." For example, "We think you just misunderstand them" or "All of us believe they're a good person." This kind of gaslighting can be even more potent as it feels harder to push back on the unanimous opinions of many.

Should you be feeling like flying monkeys are on the attack, you're not alone: it happens to a lot of us who've been unfortunate enough to have had a relationship with a narcissist. Just like many other victims of a stalker ex, I had to endure the constant attacks from the followers of my ex. don't worry. At the time, it felt endless, and it made me feel all alone in the world. I couldn't see through the fog and see the flying monkeys for what they were, but over time, I found my strength. This is where I learned how to fend off the flying monkeys, which in turn protected my sanity and sense of well-being.

1. Hold on to your reality.

Affirm and then reaffirm your own reality. You know what happened, you know how it felt to you (how could anyone else possibly tell you how a situation made you feel?) and you know what your ex is really like. A good exercise is to write some of the awful things you endured throughout the relationship down. Writing them down and even reading them aloud can affirm that what you went through really was horrific, and no one has the right to tell you otherwise or make you feel like you're exaggerating. Burn the paper afterwards - safely - if you'd like, as some kind of cathartic act.

Remember to check in with yourself from time to time, see how you're feeling and question why you may be feeling a certain way - this will help you to trust your opinions and feelings moving forward. This mentality is a great barrier for any flying monkeys trying to drag you down. The biggest weapon you have against your ex's minions is your frame of mind. You owe it to yourself to do your best to retain clarity and self-assurance.

2. Disengage from your ex and their enablers or flying monkeys

You may already be doing this, but let this point remind you to fight any temptation you may be feeling to engage with them. Even if you're itching to defend yourself or put any nasty rumors to bed, avoid engaging with them. If you do engage, they're getting the rise out of you that they desire. They, particularly your ex, will get sheer glee from you having to defend yourself against accusations and they'll revel in you getting upset over untrue rumors. Your silence will frustrate them and it'll also affirm that they're wasting their time trying to bait you. Disengage. By setting those boundaries, you give yourself mental space to be with your reality.

3. Consider therapy

I winced at this idea when it was first pitched to me. I absolutely did not want to divulge my personal life to a stranger, particularly since so many of those closest to me didn't grasp just how awful my relationship had been. But, it's worth trying. I vouch for it, especially if you have a long history of dealing with a narcissist and their cruel minions. A toxic relationship (and the nasty aftermath) can often be helped by a therapist and the safe space they offer. Your therapist will listen, they won't deny your reality. They'll let you get it all out, where it needs to be, not festering inside of you.

4. You need to stop overgiving the benefit of the doubt and second chances

You'll find that narcissist's tend to attract people into their world with relative ease; they are, after all, gifted with charisma and charm. They can be seen as fun and mysterious, which enables them to gather a merry band of followers (or, as we know them, flying monkeys). While you may have once upon a time been friendly with these minions, or perhaps you feel you still do hold some friendship connection with them, you need to be on watch once you've discovered any ties they may still hold with your ex. Once someone burns you, stop offering multiple chances, stop giving people the benefit of the doubt to your own detriment and stop being so forgiving to those who can do you harm.

That's not to say you need to toughen up and not let anyone in, but you've been burned badly - now you need to use the wisdom gained from this experience to help you navigate your future decision making. Remember this phrase: *fool me once, shame on you - fool me twice, shame on me.* Do not enable the flying monkeys by offering chances and forgiveness, even if you think they've just made a "bad choice" or didn't realize the damage they could do by going back to the narc with information. You owe it to yourself. You don't owe them anything.

Thank You For Reading

In this closing chapter, I'd like to remind you of a few things. I want you to take away a few things from this book; a sense of hope, a sense of encouragement, a newfound strength that you can overcome your abusive ex, but most of all, I want you to remember that you don't deserve this.

It's easy to become affected by an abusive ex - goodness, it's hard not to become affected by an abusive ex - but you are in control of yourself, and that's the most powerful thing you have over your abuser.

And here we are at the end of this book. I do hope it's helped you, perhaps offered some comfort to you and given you new things to think about in regards to prioritizing your safety and mental health.

I hope to pen more books after having a whole year off (I've still been writing, albeit not as much, and haven't published in over a year!) My goal is to write more consistently, and I have lists of things I endured throughout my time in a narcissistic relationship that I'd like to turn into books. As long as each book helps you and guides you in a better direction, I'll keep writing. It's cathartic for me to do, and it makes me feel good to know that I can give advice and perhaps a comfort to those who are suffering in an abusive relationship. I've come out of the other side, and I know you can, too.

Also by Lauren Kozlowski

Red Flags: The Dating Red Flag Checklist to Spot a Narcissist, Abuser or Manipulator Before They Hurt You

Narcissistic Ex

Malignant Narcissism: Understanding and Overcoming Malignant Narcissistic Abuse

Malignant Narcissism & Narcissistic Ex: 2-in-1 Collection

What a Narcissist Does at the End of a Relationship: Dealing With and Understanding the Aftermath of a Narcissistic Relationship

Narcissistic Rage: Understanding & Coping With Narcissistic Rage, Silent Treatment & Gaslighting

How to go No Contact With a Narcissist: How to Leave a Narcissist, Maintain No Contact & Break Free of the Toxic Cycle

Overcoming Narcissistic Abuse: A Four Book Collection to Guide You Through the Trauma and Help You Heal from Narcissistic Abuse

Trauma Bonding: Understanding and Overcoming the Traumatic Bond in a Narcissistic Relationship

Coercive Control: Breaking Free From Psychological Abuse

Narcissistic Stalker